Thomas Edison
Lighting a Revolution

Nick Cimarusti, M.S.

✳ Smithsonian

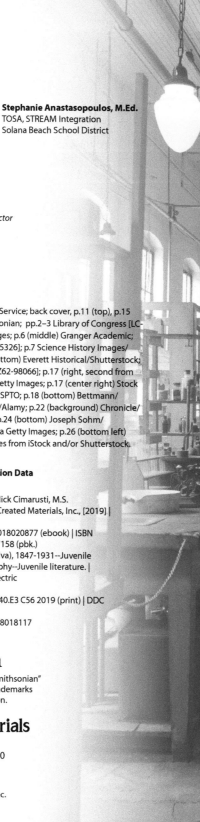

Contributing Author

Allison Duarte

Consultants

Harold D. Wallace Jr.
Curator of the Electricity Collections
National Museum of American
History

Stephanie Anastasopoulos, M.Ed.
TOSA, STREAM Integration
Solana Beach School District

Publishing Credits

Rachelle Cracchiolo, M.S.Ed., *Publisher*
Conni Medina, M.A.Ed., *Managing Editor*
Diana Kenney, M.A.Ed., NBCT, *Content Director*
Véronique Bos, *Creative Director*
Robin Erickson, *Art Director*
Michelle Jovin, M.A., *Associate Editor*
Mindy Duits, *Senior Graphic Designer*
Smithsonian Science Education Center

Image Credits: front cover, p.1 National Park Service; back cover, p.11 (top), p.15 (top), p.18 (top), p.19 (bottom), p.31 © Smithsonian; pp.2–3 Library of Congress [LC-DIG-highsm-45493] ; p.5 Keystone/Getty Images; p.6 (middle) Granger Academic; p.6 (bottom) Library of Congress [LC-USZ62-55326]; p.7 Science History Images/Alamy; p.12 Bettmann/Getty Images; p.13 (bottom) Everett Historical/Shutterstock; p.17 (bottom left) Library of Congress [LC-USZ62-98066]; p.17 (right, second from top) Oxford Science Archive/Print Collector/Getty Images; p.17 (center right) Stock Montage/Getty Images; p.17 (bottom right) USPTO; p.18 (bottom) Bettmann/Getty Images; p.21 (bottom) Randy Duchaine/Alamy; p.22 (background) Chronicle/Alamy; p.22 (top left) Jeff Morgan 05/Alamy; p.24 (bottom) Joseph Sohm/Shutterstock; p.25 (top) The Asahi Shimbun via Getty Images; p.26 (bottom left) Album/Documenta/Newscom; all other images from iStock and/or Shutterstock.

Library of Congress Cataloging-in-Publication Data

Names: Cimarusti, Nick, author.
Title: Thomas Edison : lighting a revolution / Nick Cimarusti, M.S.
Description: Huntington Beach, CA : Teacher Created Materials, Inc., [2019] |
  Audience: Grade 4 to 6. | Includes index. |
Identifiers: LCCN 2018018117 (print) | LCCN 2018020877 (ebook) | ISBN
  9781493869558 (E-book) | ISBN 9781493867158 (pbk.)
Subjects: LCSH: Edison, Thomas A. (Thomas Alva), 1847-1931--Juvenile
  literature. | Inventors--United States--Biography--Juvenile literature. |
  Light bulbs--History--Juvenile literature. | Electric
  lamps--History--Juvenile literature.
Classification: LCC TK140.E3 (ebook) | LCC TK140.E3 C56 2019 (print) | DDC
  621.32/6092 [B] --dc23
LC record available at https://lccn.loc.gov/2018018117

☼ Smithsonian

Teacher Created Materials

5301 Oceanus Drive
Huntington Beach, CA 92649-1030
www.tcmpub.com
ISBN 978-1-4938-6715-8
© 2019 Teacher Created Materials, Inc.

Table of Contents

Let There Be Light

With each new year, people look forward to a brighter future. On New Year's Eve in 1879, the future was especially bright. That evening, Thomas Edison showed off his most famous invention. Electric light bulbs lit up the night as never before.

People came from all over to see Edison's electric light bulbs. Edison and his team used the new light bulbs to light his laboratory and the surrounding buildings. Buildings were filled with light! The street could be seen clearly. A dark winter night suddenly became bright. The visitors could not believe it! There were no gas lamps in sight, just little electric bulbs. Edison created a new way to bring light into the world.

Thomas Edison did not see himself as a scientist. Edison was an inventor. What is the difference? A scientist wants to understand the world. They look for new information. But an inventor uses information to create something new. These inventions help people. Some inventions also make people money. Inventors work to **patent** their inventions.

Edison made many devices. He is most famous for his work with electricity. The electric light bulb gave people a reason to use electricity. But it was not easy getting there.

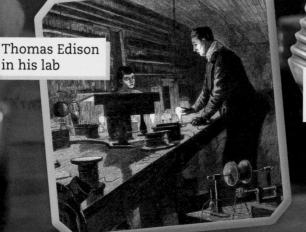

Thomas Edison in his lab

modern version of Edison's electric light bulb

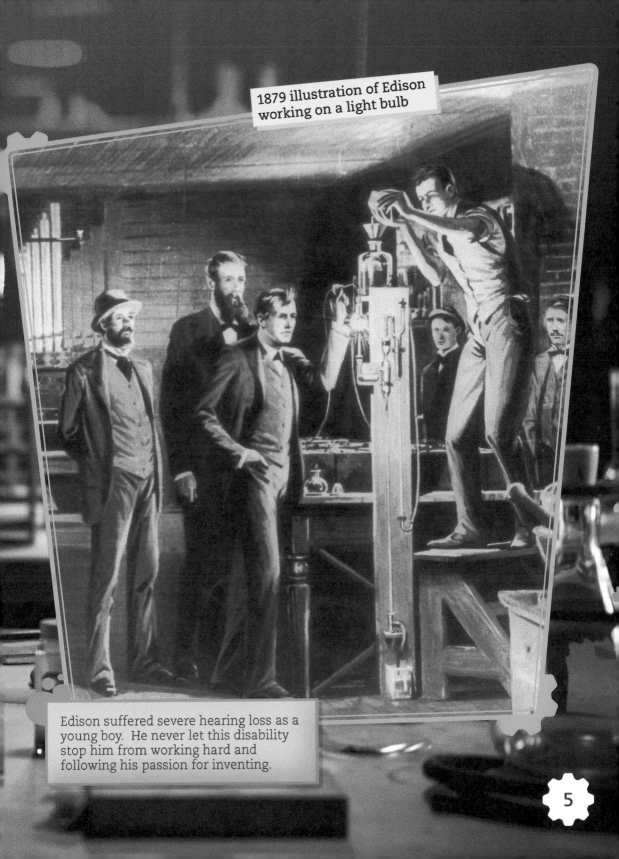

1879 illustration of Edison working on a light bulb

Edison suffered severe hearing loss as a young boy. He never let this disability stop him from working hard and following his passion for inventing.

Lighting the Way

It is no surprise that Thomas Edison was curious about the world. He loved science and experimenting. He was always looking for new information. Young Edison liked to take everything apart to understand how it worked.

At 12 years old, Edison sold newspapers and other small items, such as candy, on a train. For about six months, he even ran his own newspaper. It was called the *Weekly Herald*. His newspaper was popular with travelers on the train. Edison made enough money to build a small laboratory on the train. Once, his experiments even caused a fire!

A young Edison prints newspapers on a train.

Edison struggled in school, so his mother decided to homeschool him.

Edison to the Rescue!

When Edison was 16 years old, his life changed. One day, he was walking near the railroad when he saw a scary sight. A little boy was about to step onto the train tracks! Edison sprang into action and grabbed the boy before a train came.

The boy's father was so happy that he offered to train Edison for a new job. Edison would be a telegraph operator. It was a very important job. It required quick thinking and a lot of skill. Plus, Edison would earn more money as a telegraph operator than he did selling newspapers.

Thomas Edison tinkers with a telegraph machine.

On the Wire

Long before cell phones, telegraphs were used to talk with people who were far away. In 1844, Samuel Morse invented a practical electric telegraph. People at telegraph stations sent messages to other stations through electric wires. Operators copied the messages. All messages came in Morse code.

Morse code uses dots and dashes. Different dot-and-dash combinations stand for each letter of the alphabet. This was much faster than sending letters through the mail. News traveled with the press of a button.

Long wires were also placed along ocean floors. This helped people in different countries quickly send messages. People used the wires to talk to banks. This way, they could send money quickly.

Edison worked as an operator for four years. The job was an important one. Edison also fixed the machines. It was during this time that he learned a lot about electricity.

Edison learned about **conductors**. Electricity moves through conductors, such as wires, in a controlled manner. He learned about **insulators** too. They keep people safe from the dangerous effects of electricity. This knowledge helped Edison later in life.

These glass insulators prevent electricity from flowing between conductors.

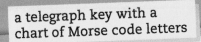
a telegraph key with a chart of Morse code letters

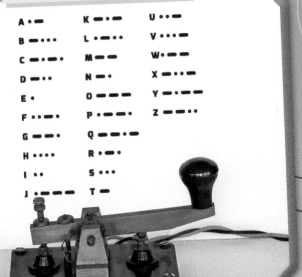

A •—	K —•—	U ••—
B —•••	L •—••	V •••—
C —•—•	M ——	W •——
D —••	N —•	X —••—
E •	O ———	Y —•——
F ••—•	P •——•	Z ——••
G ——•	Q ——•—	
H ••••	R •—•	
I ••	S •••	
J •———	T —	

SCIENCE

All Charged Up

Everything is made of tiny atoms. Each atom has a center called a nucleus, which is made of protons and neutrons. Protons have a positive charge. Electrons have a negative charge, and they circle a nucleus. Electricity flows when electrons pass their charge from one atom to another.

- electron
- neutron
- nucleus
- proton

Magic at Menlo

Edison used his new knowledge to make the telegraph even better. He invented the quadruplex system. It made it possible for four messages (two in each direction) to be sent on one wire. Before this system, only one message could be sent at a time. Sending messages became much faster.

After Edison invented his faster system, he wanted to sell it. So, he went to the Western Union Telegraph Company. It was the biggest telegraph company in the United States. The company offered him $40,000. That's more than $800,000 today! Edison could not believe it. He had a lot of money and he was only 27 years old!

With his new fortune, Edison could spend all his time inventing, which was just what he wanted. In 1876, Edison went to Menlo Park in New Jersey. There, he built what he called "The Invention Factory." There was a laboratory, a machine shop, an office, and a library.

Menlo Park was a great location. It was between New York City and Philadelphia. It was also quiet enough to complete a lot of work. Edison put together a team of some of the smartest men around. Each person had his own special skill. Some were talented scientists. Others were skilled in math and mechanics.

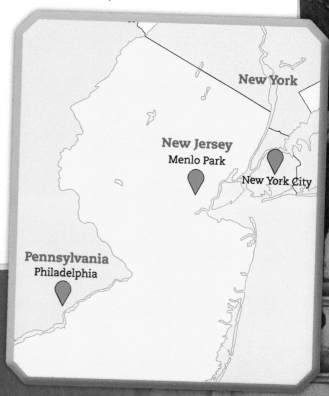

Edison and his team at Menlo Park

This illustration shows Edison in his lab at Menlo Park, when he was about 33 years old.

Menlo Park is known as the foundation of the modern research lab. There, Edison had everything he needed. He had tools, materials, and a great team. Edison and his team spent long hours working. Sometimes, they stayed up all night. Most of his team lived down the street from the lab.

Edison created some of his most famous inventions at this lab. For this reason, Edison is sometimes called the Wizard of Menlo Park. At the time, his new inventions were almost like magic!

Making Music

Edison and his team began doing other experiments with telephones. Edison wondered whether sound could be recorded and played back. He drew a design for a machine that could talk, which was known as a **phonograph**. Phonographs could record sound and play it back. Edison's design worked the first time the team tried it. That surprised the team. It even surprised Edison himself!

This invention was the early form of the record player. Later, Edison built a recording studio. Popular musicians came to Edison's lab to record their music at Menlo Park.

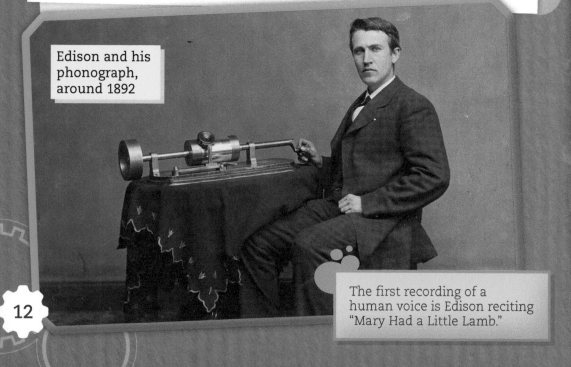

Edison and his phonograph, around 1892

The first recording of a human voice is Edison reciting "Mary Had a Little Lamb."

This illustration shows women using earphones to listen to a phonograph in New York City in 1889.

THE EDISON
CONCERT PHONOGRAPH

TRADE
Thomas A. Edison
MARK

1899 ad for a music festival

HAVE YOU HEARD IT?

A Bright Light

Edison and his team became famous. They had changed how the world communicated with a faster telegraph. Plus, their phonograph could play back recorded sound. Everyone waited for the next **ingenious** invention from Edison and his team.

All this success caught the attention of important **investors**. The Menlo Park team got enough money to work on a new project. This project would be their most important one: a practical **incandescent** light bulb.

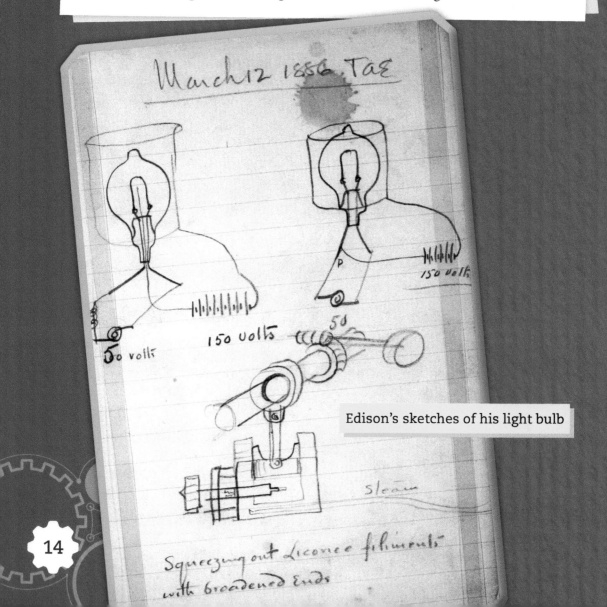

Edison's sketches of his light bulb

How Do Light Bulbs Work?

Today, light bulbs may seem like nothing special. Every home has light bulbs, but how does a light bulb actually work? Edison's light bulb was the first to use incandescence yet still be practical.

Light bulbs have four main components, or parts. First is the **filament**, which gives off light when it is heated. It took Edison many tries before he found the right material. Edison's light bulb used **carbon** as a filament.

Extra support wires are the second part of a light bulb. The wires and the filament are inside the third part, which is the glass bulb. The glass keeps all wires and gas inside the bulb in place. At the bottom of a light bulb, there is metal that conducts the electricity.

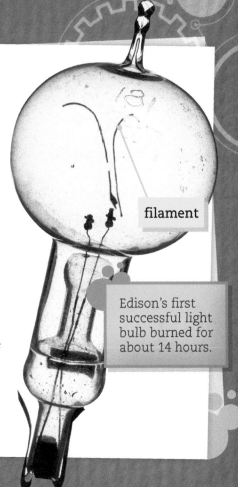

filament

Edison's first successful light bulb burned for about 14 hours.

ENGINEERING

On the Right Path

Electricity travels along a path called a **circuit**. If the path is interrupted, electricity cannot flow. This is called an open circuit. When a circuit is completely connected with no breaks, it is called a closed circuit. Flipping a light switch on is one way to complete a circuit. The closed circuit allows electricity to flow freely through wires between the light switch and the light bulb. The electricity is turned into light by the light bulb. Turn the light switch off, and the flow of electricity stops, creating an open circuit and turning off the light.

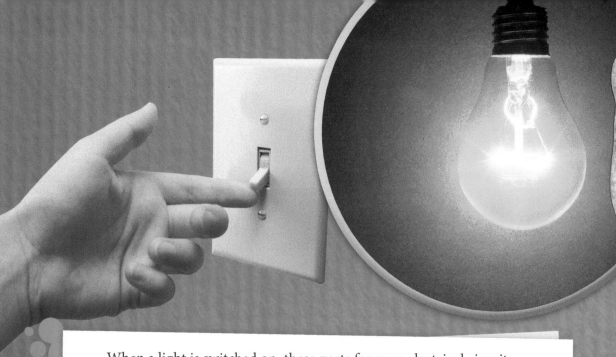

When a light is switched on, these parts form an electrical circuit. The circuit allows a **current** to flow. Currents are measured in amperes (or amps), which tell how much electricity can move through a wire. As electricity flows through the filament, the filament gets hot and glows, creating light. The power of a light bulb is measured in **wattage**. This is the product of amps and volts.

Down to the Wire

Edison did not invent the light bulb. But he made important improvements to it. His light bulbs could be used at home. They were practical. But Edison did not do all the work. Without the work of other inventors, he might not have made his discovery. Who were these others?

Alessandro Volta invented batteries. They are small and handy and easy to place inside machines. Then, Humphry Davy used a battery to create light. He called it an arc lamp.

Later, Michael Faraday combined magnets and wire. They created an electric current too. This led to **electric generators**. They used magnets and electricity to create a lot of energy. Think of them as big, powerful batteries.

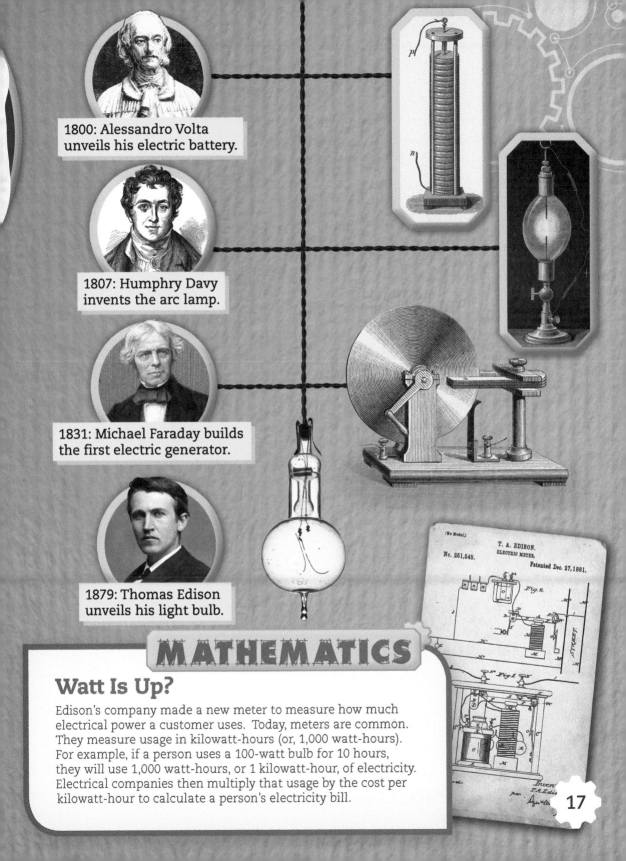

1800: Alessandro Volta unveils his electric battery.

1807: Humphry Davy invents the arc lamp.

1831: Michael Faraday builds the first electric generator.

1879: Thomas Edison unveils his light bulb.

MATHEMATICS

Watt Is Up?

Edison's company made a new meter to measure how much electrical power a customer uses. Today, meters are common. They measure usage in kilowatt-hours (or, 1,000 watt-hours). For example, if a person uses a 100-watt bulb for 10 hours, they will use 1,000 watt-hours, or 1 kilowatt-hour, of electricity. Electrical companies then multiply that usage by the cost per kilowatt-hour to calculate a person's electricity bill.

Flipping the Switch

Edison had succeeded. He solved a huge problem with electric lights. Before Edison, electric light bulbs were not practical. They were too expensive and too bright. For 60 years, inventors could not find a way to make electric light easy to use.

Outside, streetlights were electric. But they were too bright for houses. They also could not burn for very long. The light bulbs had to be replaced often. But Edison's carbon filament was a big improvement. Electric light bulbs were finally easy to use at home.

Before Edison, many homes had gas lamps. He and his team looked for ways to put electricity into homes. In New York City, Edison and his team created the Pearl Street Station. The station was a central generator of electricity. It sent electric power to buildings through a series of wires and tubes.

Changing Minds

Joseph Swan was Edison's main competition. He was an inventor too. Swan had many light bulb patents in England. He got them before Edison's big discovery. Swan's lights were not, however, as practical as Edison's. Swan and Edison eventually decided to work together. They formed a new company to share their ideas.

Joseph Swan

This engraving shows people working at Pearl Street Station.

THE ELECTRICAL AGE
March 1904

Volume XXXII Number 3
25 cents $2.50 per year

ESTABLISHED 1883

Louis Cassier, Publisher
New York and London

FROM THE FIRST PHOTOGRAPH EVER TAKEN BY INCANDESCENT ELECTRIC LAMPS. SEE PAGE 19

Electricity occurs naturally! Lightning is an electric current.

Edison's job was to convince people to switch to electric lights. People were happy with gas lights and oil lamps. Why should they change?

Edison was talented at promoting his work. He gave people a reason to care. He talked to newspapers to spread the word. He even modeled his electrical wiring system after the familiar gas system. A central source would send power to homes using paths that cut through cities and towns. These paths were electrical conductors, called **mains**.

Edison also showed off his work. He had to be a salesman if he wanted his light bulbs to be successful. The New Year's Eve party at Menlo Park was his first big demonstration. Then, Edison's electric lights were used on a new steamship, the S.S. *Columbia*. The lights were a big success.

Slowly but surely, electricity replaced gas. In London, there was even the first use of an electric sign, spelling out "Edison."

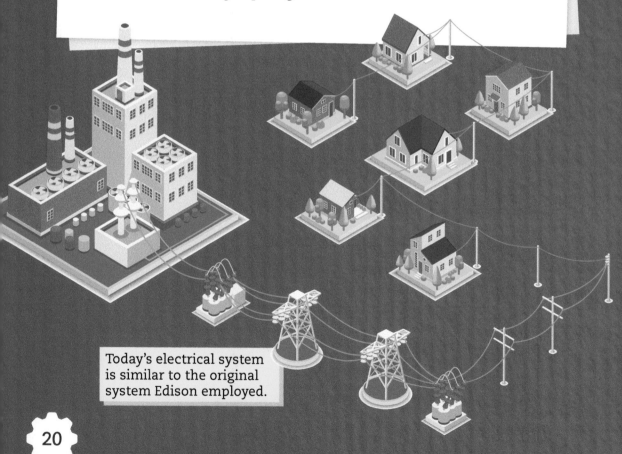

Today's electrical system is similar to the original system Edison employed.

Edison (right) and the founder of Kodak, George Eastman, operate a motion picture camera around 1925.

Until 2003, Edison held the record for most patented inventions.

kinetograph

Lights, Camera, Action!

Edison also helped invent movies. Remember the phonograph? Inspired by this, Edison wanted to record images. His kinetograph did just that.

It was a motion picture camera. The camera took pictures very fast and put them on a long strip. Edison even built his own small movie studio. Soon, the first movie theater was playing short films in New York City.

ELECTRIC Cookery
will halve your kitchen work –

save food, and tempt you to pre-
pare many a good dish not w...
the trouble by old-fashi...
methods.

The comfort of the ho...
hold is measured by the
smooth working of the
kitchen, for this an Electric
Range is essential. So cheap
to run—just one unit of
Electricity per person per day.

Your Local ELECTRIC
AGENT will tell you all
about Electric Ranges.

SWITCH ON TO HEALTH

For Health's Sake – USE ELECTRICITY

H. 30.

1928 ad for electric stoves

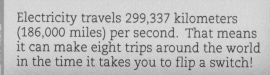

Electricity travels 299,337 kilometers
(186,000 miles) per second. That means
it can make eight trips around the world
in the time it takes you to flip a switch!

Lighting the World

As everyone switched to electricity, even more changes happened. More power stations were built. Homes and buildings added wiring. With this wiring came new gadgets. Offices and kitchens would never be the same.

The use of electricity let people have control over simple things in their lives. Electric lights allowed rooms to be bright at any time of day. People got news instantly at home with radios. Friends used the telephone to say hello. Workers could work longer hours. Skyscrapers were possible thanks to electric elevators.

People bought electric vacuums and washing machines. They used toasters and fans. Electric lights replaced candles when celebrating holidays. Suddenly, everything was electric!

People saved candles for when the power went out during "blackouts." Even then, flashlights had become an option. Cities could be bright all day and all night. The world felt brand new.

Honoring Edison

Edison did not stop with his light bulb. He invented until his death. His passion was to invent, and he never lost sight of it.

Thomas Edison died on October 18, 1931. Four nights later, President Herbert Hoover asked Americans to turn off their lights at 10 p.m. eastern standard time. All across the country, a moment of darkness honored Thomas Edison's brilliance.

A Bright Future

The light bulb continued to improve. Edison's company had **merged** with another company to form General Electric (GE) in 1892. Inventors at the company kept making small changes to create better light bulbs.

Over the years, different materials improved the light bulb. In 1910, a researcher named William Coolidge used **tungsten** instead of carbon. This metal burned brighter and used less energy. It could be made thinner than a strand of hair. This led to lights that could go in cars and trains.

By 1940, GE had made **fluorescent** light bulbs. They were very expensive to make at first, but they used much less energy than incandescent light bulbs. With time, they improved and became cheaper to make. Eventually they even began to appear in homes.

Today, many people use light-emitting diodes, or LEDs. These lights are even more **efficient** than fluorescent light bulbs. LEDs are very bright and can be used almost anywhere. Soon, LED bulbs might be the most popular type of light bulb.

Fun in the Sun

Energy efficiency is now the goal of all light bulbs. That is why some homes have started to use solar panels. Thin layers of conductive material change sunlight into electric currents. Solar panels have the potential to save money. They are also better for the planet.

Solar panels convert sunlight to electricity.

Electricity is used.

Electricity is brought in from power lines when needed.

Extra electricity is sent to power lines.

Nobel Prize winners Isamu Akasaki, Hiroshi Amano, and Shuji Nakamura

TECHNOLOGY

Out of the Blue

LED bulbs use less energy than incandescent ones, plus, they burn brighter for longer. But they were a by-product! Nick Holonyak Jr. made an LED laser in 1962. Soon, others used this invention to create a general purpose light. In the early 1990s, inventors created blue LEDs, which could then be combined with red and green to form white LEDs. One American and two Japanese inventors shared the 2014 Nobel Prize for different parts of that research.

Seeing the Light

Thomas Edison is an important person in history. To this day, a light bulb is the symbol for a good idea. Edison was always curious about the world. He asked questions. He took things apart and put them back together.

His genius still affects us today. Look above you. That light is because of Edison. The movie you saw last night? Thank Edison. That song you heard? It was Edison too.

Edison believed in using failure as a chance to learn. Not every invention was a success. But every time he failed, he learned how to make things better. Edison's life is evidence that everything can be improved. That's why he was so successful! He learned to invent things people needed.

Take Charge

Edison once said, "Genius is 99 percent **perspiration** and 1 percent inspiration." You have probably heard some version of this advice. Edison provides an example of how far hard work can take you.

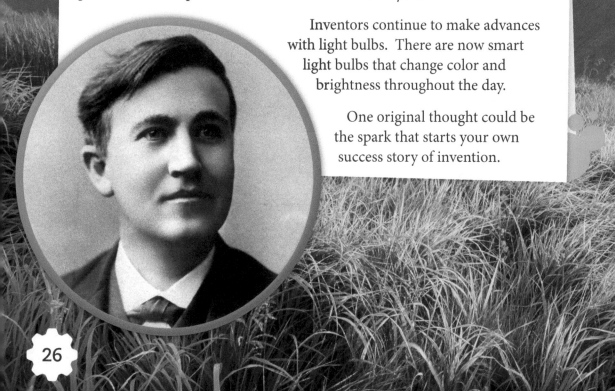

Inventors continue to make advances with light bulbs. There are now smart light bulbs that change color and brightness throughout the day.

One original thought could be the spark that starts your own success story of invention.

A homeowner changes the color and brightness of his light bulb.

ARTS

Cut It Out

On a roof, solar panels can absorb more energy by following the sun as it moves. But the devices used to create this motion are heavy and expensive. Researchers want to use *kirigami* to solve this problem. *Kirigami* is the Japanese art of paper folding and cutting. This technique could make the panels lighter and more efficient.

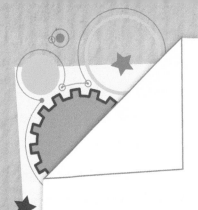

STEAM CHALLENGE

Define the Problem

Electricity is in limited supply in some parts of the world. People in these areas have turned to solar ovens for cooking and heating water to make it safe for drinking. You are part of an engineering team that will introduce a solar oven design and materials to a community in Kenya. Your task is to design and build an effective way to capture energy from the sun.

Constraints: Your model must be easy to reproduce and should be made with three materials or fewer.

Criteria: Your solar oven must increase the temperature of 50 milliliters (10 teaspoons) of water by 5° Celsius (9° Fahrenheit).

Research and Brainstorm

What types of materials and colors would be most useful in a solar oven? How can you use Edison's inventing failures as inspiration?

Design and Build

Sketch your solar oven design. What purpose will each part serve? What materials will work best? Build the model.

Test and Improve

Place 50 mL (10 tsp.) of water and a thermometer in the oven. Place the oven in an outdoor area with direct sunlight. Record the temperature of the water every 5 minutes for 20 minutes. Did it work? How can you improve it? Modify your design and try again.

Reflect and Share

Compare your team's design to other designs in the class. How is your team's design similar and different? What can you learn from other designs? Why is it important for scientists and engineers to share their work?

Glossary

carbon—a chemical element that is found in petroleum and in all living plants and animals

circuit—the complete path of an electric current

conductors—materials that allow electricity to flow

current—the flow of electricity in motion

efficient—productive without wasting time or resources

electric generators—machines with magnets and conductors that create electricity

filament—a thin strip of thread-like material

fluorescent—producing light when electricity flows through a gas-filled tube

incandescent—glowing with heat

ingenious—very clever

insulators—materials that block the flow of sound, electricity, or heat

investors—people who give money to start a company and get stocks or profit in return

mains—systems of pipes or circuits used to deliver utilities

merged—joined together

patent—to obtain an official guarantee for an inventor to be the only one to make, use, and sell their invention

perspiration—sweat

phonograph—a device used for playing musical records

tungsten—a hard metal

wattage—the amount of electricity something uses

Index

Do you want to be an inventor?
Here are some tips to get you started.

"I am fascinated when an inventor takes a simple idea, and, through ingenuity and persistence, creates a practical device. If you love being inventive and creative, along with a science and history background, you too could become a famous inventor."
—*Bernard S. Finn, Curator*

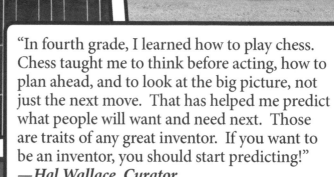

"In fourth grade, I learned how to play chess. Chess taught me to think before acting, how to plan ahead, and to look at the big picture, not just the next move. That has helped me predict what people will want and need next. Those are traits of any great inventor. If you want to be an inventor, you should start predicting!"
—*Hal Wallace, Curator*